PENGUIN READERS

Dear Parents and Educators,

Welcome to Penguin Readers! As parents and educators, you know that each child develops at their own pace—in terms of speech, critical thinking, and, of course, reading. As a result, each Penguin Readers book is assigned an easy-to-read level (1–4), detailed below. Penguin Readers features esteemed authors and illustrators, stories about favorite characters, fascinating nonfiction, and more!

EMERGENT READER
Simple vocabulary • Word repetition • Picture clues • Predictable story and sentence structures • Familiar themes and ideas

PROGRESSING READER
Longer sentences • Simple dialogue • Picture and context clues • More in-depth plot development • Nonfiction and fiction

TRANSITIONAL READER
Multisyllable and compound words • More dialogue • Different points of view • More complex storylines and characters • Greater range of genres

FLUENT READER
More advanced vocabulary • Detailed and descriptive text • Complex sentence structure • In-depth plot and character development • Full range of genres

*This book has been officially leveled by using the F&P Text Level Gradient™ leveling system.

To Autumn and Austin, you mean the world to me. Thank you for keeping me joyful and curious—JB

PENGUIN YOUNG READERS
An imprint of Penguin Random House LLC
1745 Broadway, New York, New York 10019

First published in the United States of America by Penguin Young Readers,
an imprint of Penguin Random House LLC, 2025

TIME for Kids © 2025 TIME USA, LLC. All Rights Reserved.

Photo credits: cover, 3: Valentin Baciu/iStock/Getty Images; front flap: Jasius/Moment/Getty Images; 4: Wirestock/iStock/Getty Images; 5: marcouliana/iStock/Getty Images; 6: blueringmedia/iStock/Getty Images; 7: (left) Leila Coker/iStock/Getty Images, (right) Smithore/iStock/Getty Images; 8: Martin Anderson/500px/Getty Images; 9: (top) GlassEyeStock/iStock/Getty Images, (bottom) TrichopCMU/iStock/Getty Images; 10–11: Sebastian/Adobe Stock; 12: Premaphotos/Alamy Stock Photo; 13: Chris Minihane/Moment Open/Getty Images; 14: wisan224/iStock/Getty Images; 15: heckepics/iStock/Getty Images; 16: Frans Sellies/Moment Open/Getty Images; 17: Anne-Marie Palmer/Alamy Stock Photo; 18: Klaus Nicodem/iStock/Getty Images; 19: Paul Starosta/Stone/Getty Images; 20: Jojo Dexter/iStock/Getty Images; 21: Valter Jacinto/Moment/Getty Images; 22: hawk111/iStock/Getty Images; 23: (top) Darkdiamond67/iStock/Getty Images, (bottom, left) Nigel Harris/iStock/Getty Images, (bottom, right) piemags/nature/Alamy Stock Photo; 24: Heather Burditt/iStock/Getty Images; 25: Laszlo Podor/Moment/Getty Images; 27: Koichi Yoshii/iStock/Getty Images; 28: Jasius/Moment/Getty Images; 29: Lubo Ivanko/iStock/Getty Images; 30: JMrocek/iStock/Getty Images; 31: Ian Fox/iStock/Getty Images; 32: Gins Wang/E+/Getty Images

Penguin Random House values and supports copyright. Copyright fuels creativity, encourages diverse voices, promotes free speech, and creates a vibrant culture. Thank you for buying an authorized edition of this book and for complying with copyright laws by not reproducing, scanning, or distributing any part of it in any form without permission. You are supporting writers and allowing Penguin Random House to continue to publish books for every reader. Please note that no part of this book may be used or reproduced in any manner for the purpose of training artificial intelligence technologies or systems.

Visit us online at penguinrandomhouse.com.

Library of Congress Cataloging-in-Publication Data is available.

Manufactured in China

ISBN 9780593888049 (pbk)   10 9 8 7 6 5 4 3 2 1 WKT
ISBN 9780593888056 (hc)   10 9 8 7 6 5 4 3 2 1 WKT

The publisher does not have any control over and does not assume any responsibility for author or third-party websites or their content.

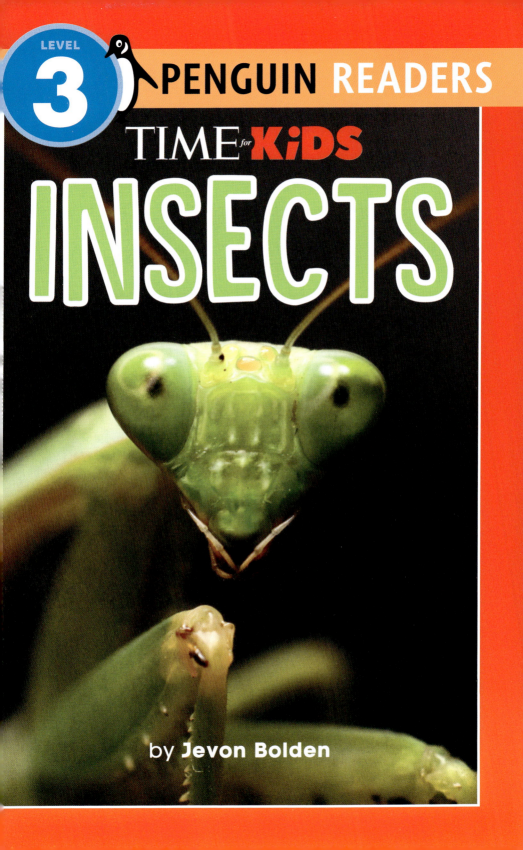

LEVEL 3

PENGUIN READERS

TIME for KiDS

INSECTS

by Jevon Bolden

Insects are some of the most important creatures on this planet. They help keep Earth's ecosystem in balance.

Insects such as bees, flower flies, and butterflies pollinate flowering plants, supplying us with honey and our fields with more flowers. They also pollinate agricultural crops that provide food for humans and animals. Lacewings keep agricultural pests such as aphids and mites from eating and destroying crops.

Dragonflies help control populations of

disease-carrying bugs, such as mosquitoes.

Beetles remove waste from the environment by eating organic waste, such as animal feces. Removal of organic waste keeps down the spread of pathogens (organisms such as viruses and bacteria that cause diseases).

Insects come in many shapes, sizes, and colors. From iridescent beetles to mantises that look like flowers, the world is full of insects whose stunning colors and unique shapes serve a purpose for their survival and our planet's well-being.

Insects are invertebrates, which means they do not have a backbone. They always have six legs and a three-part body made up of a head, a thorax, and an abdomen.

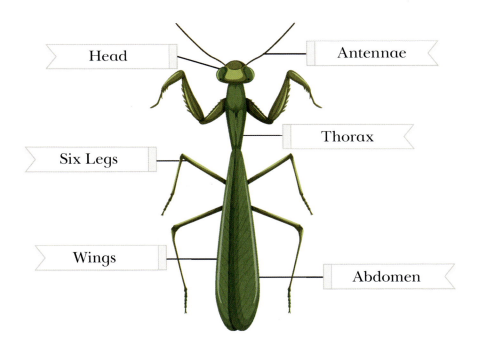

Some insects have wings. These include bees, wasps, butterflies, dragonflies, and some beetles.

Not only are there many kinds of insects but there are also many, many individual insects alive right now. There are about ten quintillion (10,000,000,000,000,000,000) insects on Earth!

Insects are sometimes referred to as *bugs*, but not everything that you might call a bug is an insect.

Spiders are not insects. They are arachnids. Spiders have eight legs, two main body parts (a cephalothorax—a combination of the head and thorax—and an abdomen), and no wings.

Centipedes and millipedes aren't insects, either. They have many body segments and more than six legs.

Now let's check out some of the world's most unique and vibrant insects.

The striking looks of the spiny flower mantis allow it to camouflage itself among flowers and leaves. It's a small mantis, about one and a half inches long, and is native to southern and eastern Africa. Two of its wings have black-and-yellow swirls that almost look like the eyes of a larger animal. When it is threatened, the spiny flower mantis raises its wings to show its "eyes," which scares away predators.

The back of a Picasso bug looks like something you might see in an art museum! This bug uses its vibrant colors to scare away predators and stay safe. Like a stink bug, it releases a bad smell when it is disturbed or crushed. Picasso bugs live in tropical and subtropical Africa and eat plants. They can reach a length of more than half an inch.

Can you guess how this next insect got its name?

The orchid mantis has a yellow or pink-and-white body, and its flat legs resemble flower petals. It can grow as long as two and a half inches.

Found in tropical forests from India to Indonesia, this praying mantis not only looks like a flower but also often lives near flowers. It blends in with the blooms, and stays hidden from both prey and predators.

The emerald swallowtail is a shade-shifting butterfly. It has dark green wings with bright bands of color on them that look different in different light. From one angle, the bands are light green. From another angle, the bands look yellow or blue.

The other side of its wings look completely different: They are black and gray with blue, orange, and white spots. All this color changing helps this butterfly stay safe from harm.

The emerald swallowtail has an average wingspan of four inches. It is native to Southeast Asia but can be found in butterfly houses around the world.

The rare rainbow leaf beetle can be found in forests throughout Europe and is classified as endangered in the United Kingdom. It's no surprise where it got its name: Its shiny body is covered in streaks of red, green, and purple. The rainbow leaf beetle loves to eat wild thyme and can grow to almost half an inch.

Wasps are among the top three deadliest bugs to humans on the planet. The iridescent cuckoo wasp is a predator, but unlike other wasps, it doesn't sting. Instead, it is a kind of parasite. It survives by taking over other wasps' nests and laying its own eggs in them. The cuckoo wasp's babies (or larvae) then eat the other wasps' eggs and their food.

With its sculptured and highly colorful body, the cuckoo wasp can be found almost everywhere in the world, except Antarctica. Adult cuckoo wasps are small, often not growing larger than half an inch long.

Dragonflies and damselflies are often mistaken for each other. But there are key differences that set these curious creatures apart.

While each can be found near shallow, fresh water almost anywhere in the world, dragonflies have eyes closer together and bulkier bodies than damselflies, and damselflies have more space between their eyes. Dragonflies can have wingspans between about one and six inches, and damselflies' wingspans range from half an inch to seven and a half inches. And while damselflies fold their wings when they are not flying, dragonflies at rest keep their wings straight out by their sides like an airplane.

However, both feed on other insects and come in bright colors like green, blue, pink, red, and more.

Crimson marsh glider

Common blue damselfly

Hawaiian upland damselfly

The smallest of the world's silk moths, the rosy maple moth is draped in soft and fuzzy pinks, yellows, and purples. Its wingspan ranges from one and a half to two and a half inches. This tiny creature is found in North America, and as a caterpillar, its diet consists mainly of maple leaves. That's where it gets its name.

The jewel beetle (also known as the metallic wood-borer beetle) is considered one of the most colorful insects in the world. There are about 15,000 species of them that live in North America, Thailand, and other parts of Southeast Asia. Appearing in colors like red, green, blue, and purple, the most vibrantly colored large beetles in this species are favorites of many insect collectors. Their colorful shells are sometimes used for making beetle-wing jewelry. They make their homes in areas with lots of trees and plants and can cause serious damage by eating through orchards, shrubs, and forest trees.

This shiny bug can grow to a length of about one to two inches.

Known as the comet moth or the Madagascan moon moth, this bright yellow-and-red insect can be found in the rainforests of Madagascar, off the southeastern coast of Africa. It has an impressive wingspan of up to eight inches.

After these moths emerge from their cocoons, their mouths and digestive systems no longer work. And since they can't eat, they live for only six to eight days.

The comet moth uses its long red-and-yellow tails as a defense against attackers, such as bats. The tails spin, interfering with the bat's echolocation and leading it to attack the tails instead of the body of the moth.

Why are insects so many different colors and shapes? It's not just to stand out. These varying looks also work to keep them safe from attacks or help them hunt for food. Some flash their colors to warn predators that they are poisonous and will taste bad. Others use their colors to attract mates.

Bugs are often creatures that people ignore or are afraid of. But when you  take time to look a little closer, their real magic appears.

Glittering gold, incredible iridescence, and radiant rainbows adorn our featured insects. These attributes are cool to look at, and they are evidence of how different kinds of creatures have adapted over time. Bugs might be small, but they have a big impact on our world!

Which insect is your favorite?